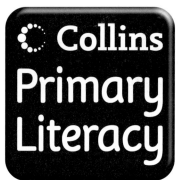

Pupil Book 2

Karina Law
Series editor: Kay Hiatt

Published by Collins
An imprint of HarperCollins*Publishers*
77–85 Fulham Palace Road
Hammersmith
London
W6 8JB

© HarperCollins*Publishers* Limited 2008

Series editor: Kay Hiatt

10 9 8 7

ISBN 978 0 00 722696 2

Karina Law asserts her moral right to be identified as the author of this work.

British Library Cataloguing in Publication Data
A Catalogue record for this publication is available from the British Library.

Acknowledgements
The author and publishers wish to thank the following for permission to use copyright material:
Unit 1: Orion Group for text and illustrations from *Horrid Henry's Perfect Day* by Francesca Simon from *Horrid Henry*, text © Francesca Simon, 1994, illustrations © Tony Ross, 1994, Horrid Henry is a registered trademark (Orion Children's Books); HarperCollins for text and illustrations from *Class Six and the Very Big Rabbit* by Martin Waddell, text © Martin Waddell, 2005, illustrations © Tony Ross, 2005 (Collins Big Cat); Unit 2: Usborne Publishing Limited for text and illustrations from *I Can Cut and Stick* by Ray Gibson, © Usborne Publishing Limited; Usborne Publishing Limited for text and illustrations from *Kitchen Fun* by Ray Gibson, © Usborne Publishing Limited; Unit 3: Jacqueline Brown for use of "Street Sounds" by Jacqueline Brown from *Another Very First Poetry Book* compiled by John Foster, text © Jacqueline Brown, 1992 (Oxford University Press); Dave Ward for use of "We Want to Wear Our Wellies" by Dave Ward from *The Works* edited by Paul Cookson, text © Dave Ward (Macmillan); Unit 4: Margaret Carter for text from *A Kiss from a Princess* retold by Margaret Carter from *The Story of the Frog Prince*, text © Margaret Carter, 1991 (Kingfisher Nursery Chest); Penguin Books for text and illustrations from *The Frog Prince Continued* by Jon Scieszka from *The Frog Prince Continued*, text © Jon Scieszka, 1991, illustrations © Steve Johnson, 1991 (Puffin); Penguin Books for text and illustrations from *The Other Frog Prince* by Jon Scieszka from *The Stinky Cheese Man and Other Fairly Stupid Tales*, text © Jon Scieszka, 1992, illustrations © Lane Smith, 1992 (Viking); Unit 5: Usborne Publishing Limited for text and illustrations from *Beginners: Eggs and Chicks* by Fiona Patchett, © Usborne Publishing Limited, 1992; Unit 6: PFD on behalf of the author for use of "Hot Food" by Michael Rosen from *The Hypnotiser*, text © Michael Rosen, 1988 (Scholastic); HarperCollins USA for use of "Spaghetti! Spaghetti!" by Jack Prelutsky from *Rainy Rainy Saturday*, text © Jack Prelutsky, 1980; Unit 7: Pamela Todd Literary Agent for text from *The Last Noo-Noo* by Jill Murphy, text © Jill Murphy, 1995 (Walker Books); Pamela Todd Literary Agent for text from *The Worst Witch* by Jill Murphy, text © Jill Murphy, 1974 (Puffin); Pamela Todd Literary Agent for text from *Author profile* from The Book Trust; Unit 8: Usborne Publishing Limited for text and illustrations from *Beginners: Eggs and Chicks* by Fiona Patchett, © Usborne Publishing Limited; Unit 9: "Breakfast for One" by Judith Nicholls, text © Judith Nicholls, 2000 (Macmillan) reprinted with kind permission of the author; Eddison Pearson on behalf of the author for use of "Teatime" by Valerie Bloom from *Let Me Touch the Sky, Selected Poems for Children* by Valerie Bloom; Tony Mitton for use of "Teaser" by Tony Mitton from *Groovy Greek Hero Raps* by Tony Mitton (Orchard); Unit 10: HarperCollins for text and illustrations from *Mountain Mona* by Vivian French, text © Vivian French, 2006, illustrations © Chris Fisher, 2006 (Collins Big Cat); Unit 11: Penguin Books for text from *Munching, Crunching, Sniffing and Snooping* by Brian Moses, © Dorling Kindersley, 1999 (Dorling Kindersley); Hodder & Stoughton for text and illustrations from *Our Senses: Taste* by Kay Woodward (Hodder Wayland)

Illustrations: Shirley Chiang, Sarah Horne, Gemma Hastilow, Julian Mosedale, Liz Toole

Photographs: p34, top: FLPA/David Hosking, bottom: photolibrary.com/Zigmund Leszczynski; p35, top: NHPA/Anthony Bannister, middle: photolibrary.com/Zigmund Leszczynski, bottom: NHPA/Anthony Bannister; p36, middle: Alamy/Mark Sykes; p38, top right: npl.com/Jose B. Ruiz, middle: Alamy/Papilio, bottom right: Alamy/Roger Eritja, bottom left: npl.com/Delpho/ARCO; p39, top right: npl.com/Delpho/ARCO; p40, bottom middle: Robert Pickett/Corbis, bottom right: Julie Habel/Corbis; p57, bottom right: Pamela Todd Literary Agent; p88, top left: Jerry Young/Dorling Kindersley, top right: Jerry Young/Dorling Kindersley, middle: Jerry Young/Dorling Kindersley, bottom left: Jerry Young/Dorling Kindersley, bottom right: Planet Earth/Getty Images; p89, all: Jerry Young/Dorling Kindersley; p90, top right: Marty Snyderman/SeaPics.com, middle: Jerry Young/Dorling Kindersley, bottom: Jerry Young/Dorling Kindersley; p92, bottom right: Hodder Wayland Picture Library; p93, top: Corbis, bottom: Getty Images

Every effort has been made to trace copyright holders and to obtain their permission for the use of copyright material. The authors and publishers will gladly receive any information enabling them to rectify any error or omission in subsequent editions.

Browse the complete Collins catalogue at
www.collinseducation.com

Printed in Hong Kong by Printing Express Ltd

Mixed Sources
Product group from well-managed
forests and other controlled sources
www.fsc.org Cert no. SW-COC-1806
© 1996 Forest Stewardship Council

FSC is a non-profit international organisation established to promote the responsible management of the world's forests. Products carrying the FSC label are independently certified to assure consumers that they come from forests that are managed to meet the social, economic and ecological needs of present and future generations.

Find out more about HarperCollins and the environment at
www.harpercollins.co.uk/green

Contents

Perfectly Horrid

In this unit, you'll read from different stories with familiar settings and then write a story of your own.

Horrid Henry's Perfect Day

This story is about two brothers who are very different from each other.

Henry was horrid.

Everyone said so, even his mother.

Henry threw food, Henry snatched, Henry pushed and shoved and pinched. Even his teddy avoided him when possible.

His parents despaired.

"What are we going to do about that horrid boy?" sighed Mum.

"How did two people as nice as us have such a horrid child?" sighed Dad.

When Horrid Henry's parents took Henry to school they walked behind him and pretended he was not theirs.

Children pointed at Henry and whispered to their parents, "That's Horrid Henry."

"He's the boy who threw my jacket in the mud."

"He's the boy who squashed Billy's beetle."

"He's the boy who…" Fill in whatever terrible deed you like. Horrid Henry was sure to have done it.

Horrid Henry had a younger brother. His name was Perfect Peter.

Perfect Peter always said "Please" and "Thank you". Perfect Peter loved vegetables.

Perfect Peter always used a hankie and never, ever picked his nose.

"Why can't you be perfect like Peter?" said Horrid Henry's mum every day.

As usual, Henry pretended not to hear. He continued melting Peter's crayons on the radiator.

But Horrid Henry started to think.

"What if *I* were perfect?" thought Henry. "I wonder what would happen."

from **Horrid Henry** *by Francesca Simon*

1 Responding to the text

Answer the questions from the  or section.

① Write down three horrid things that Henry does.

② What did Henry do to Billy's beetle?

③ What is Henry's younger brother called?

④ What sort of things might Henry do if he were perfect instead of horrid?

① Why did Henry's parents walk behind him on the way to school?

② What did Henry's brother think of vegetables?

③ What did Henry do with Peter's crayons?

④ Look at each of these words and write down a word that means the opposite.

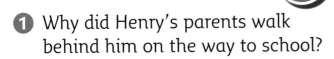

horrid   nice   kind   tidy   rude

① What's the worst thing that Henry has done? Why do you think that?

② Mum asks Henry why he can't be perfect, like Peter. Why do you think Henry pretends not to hear?

③ What do you think will happen next?

④ Use a thesaurus to find words that mean the same as *horrid* and *perfect*.

2 Role play

In groups of four, pretend that Henry's teacher has called Henry and his parents in to school to discuss his horrid behaviour. Decide who'll play each part.

The scene could start with the teacher describing some of the terrible things Henry has done.

3 Think/pair/share

In pairs, think of some questions you would like to ask Horrid Henry.

- What do you think of your brother?

- Do you like school?

4 Saying you're sorry!

Pretend you're Henry. Write a letter of apology to one of the other characters.

- You could write to Billy to say sorry for squashing his beetle.

- You could write a card to Henry's teacher to say that you're sorry.

Write a contract for good behaviour for Henry. Make it clear how he should behave and what will happen if he doesn't!

5 Words and pictures

Work in a group. Choose one of these sets of characters.
Talk about the characters in the set you've chosen.
Write down lists of words that describe them.

Share your words with another group. Can they think of
more words?

Add any of the words that you like the sound of to your
own lists.

Class Six and the Very Big Rabbit

Class Six have a very special teacher. When she wiggles her ears,
all sorts of strange things can happen.

Class Six liked their teacher, Miss Bennett. She could do magic,
like no one else could. She could wiggle her ears and make things
disappear. Then she'd earwiggle again, and make them come back.

One day she did something different. She was reading Class Six
a book about rabbits.

"Rabbits *are* nice," Miss Bennett said.
Then she grinned and earwiggled.
"I wish I was a rabbit!" she said.

And... there was a fizzzz...
and a flash...
and a bang...

...and Miss Bennett changed
into a very big rabbit.

Class Six sat and looked
at the very big rabbit, and the
very big rabbit sat looking right
back at Class Six.

She was Miss Bennett-sized, and she had glasses like Miss
Bennett. She was holding the book Miss Bennett had been reading,
so Class Six knew it had to be her. They just didn't know how she
had managed the trick.

Everyone cheered the big rabbit.

The big rabbit went back to the rabbit book and started reading
again. At least she tried to read, but all that came out were squeaks.

"Rabbits can't read," Ranjit whispered to Rachel.

"You can't blame her for trying," Rachel whispered back.

"It's a cool trick, Miss Bennett," Ranjit told the big rabbit politely. "The best trick that I've ever seen, but we think it's time you went back to being Miss Bennett."

The big rabbit earwiggled again, and she squeaked.

"Something's gone wrong with the wishing!" Ranjit whispered to Rachel.

"I don't think she knows what to do," Rachel said.

The big rabbit froze.

"That's what rabbits do when they're caught, and can't think of a way to escape," Ranjit told Rachel. "Miss Bennett's got stuck as a rabbit and doesn't know how to wish herself back."

from **Class Six and the Very Big Rabbit** *by Martin Waddell (Collins Big Cat)*

6 Responding to the text

Answer the questions from the   or section.

1 What did Miss Bennett wish for?

2 What happened when Miss Bennett made her wish?

3 What happened when the rabbit tried to read to Class Six?

4 If you could change into something else, what would you choose to be? Why?

1 In what ways was Miss Bennett different from other teachers?

2 How did Class Six react when their teacher turned into a rabbit?

3 How did Class Six know that the rabbit was Miss Bennett?

4 What do you think will happen next?

7 Think/pair/share

Plan a story about a teacher who turns into a creature. With your partner, think about these questions:

- **Where** does the story take place?

- **Who** is in the story?

- **What** unexpected thing will happen?

- **How** will the story end?

8 Making a storyboard

This storyboard shows what happens in *Class Six and the Very Big Rabbit.*

Beginning	Middle	End

The teacher turns into a rabbit.	Class Six try to think of a way to change her back.	**?**

❶ Talk with your partner about what happens at the end of *Class Six and the Very Big Rabbit.*

❷ In pairs, make a storyboard to show what happens at the beginning, middle and end of *your* story.

9 Writing your story

Follow these steps to write your story.

- **Beginning** – What sort of creature will the teacher in your story turn into?

- **Middle** – What sort of problems will the creature cause?

- **Ending** – How will your story end? Will the creature change back into a teacher or will something else happen?

Remember!

- Use interesting words and phrases to describe your characters.

- Think how the children will react when their teacher changes.

What I have learned

- I can talk about the setting and characters in stories I've read.

- I can plan a story with an extraordinary character in an ordinary setting.

- I can write a well organised, interesting story.

Take a Paper Plate

In this unit, you'll read and follow instructions, and write instructions for making a mask.

Make an Octopus Puppet

Take a paper plate – and turn it into something completely different!

❶ Cut a paper plate like this. You need both pieces.

❷ Turn the big piece over. Use a sponge to wipe green paint all over.

❸ Wipe green paint on both sides of a sheet of strong paper. Roll it up.

❹ Cut the roll into pieces, like this. Then unroll them.

5 Stick them to the unpainted side of the plate.

6 Tape the small piece of plate to the back, for a handle.

Stick on paper eyes and a mouth.

You can add some patterns to your octopus.

from **I Can Cut and Stick** *by Ray Gibson*

1 Making an octopus puppet

1 Follow the instructions to make the octopus puppet.

2 Think of three things that make the instructions easy to follow.

Make a Pecking Bird

Take another paper plate – and make it into an exotic bird.

① Fold a paper plate. Unfold. Paint stripes on the back.

② Fold it again. Stick a paper beak inside.

③ Cut some paper into spikes.

④ Stick them on the head. Add an eye.

⑤ Cut strips of bright tissue as long as your hand.

⑥ Twist them together. Tape them at the back for a tail.

Cut feather shapes and stick them on if you like.

Rock your bird to make it peck.

from **I Can Cut and Stick** *by Ray Gibson*

2 Responding to the text

Answer the questions from the or   section.

❶ What is the bird's body made of?

❷ What is its tail made of?

❸ Write a list of the things you'll need to make a pecking bird.

❶ How do you make the bird peck?

❷ What else could you use if you didn't have a paper plate?

❸ Make a list of the words that start each instruction. For example, *fold*, *unfold*, *paint*.

Cress Creatures – Woolly Sheep

These sheep are fun to grow.

You will need:		
	• cress seeds	• a jug of cold water
	• a dinner plate	• brown or black felt or paper
	• scissors	• a scrap of white felt or paper
	• cotton wool	• a black felt-tip pen

1 Pull some cotton wool into a rough shape for the sheep's body and lay it on a plate.

2 Cut out some ears, a face and some legs in black felt and lay them on the cotton wool.

3 Cut the eyes out of white felt and mark in the centre with a black felt-tip pen.

4 Add some extra cotton wool for the forehead and tail.

5 Wet the cotton wool.

6 Sprinkle some cress seeds over the cotton wool.

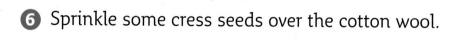

7 Keep the cotton wool and cress moist by pouring a little water onto the plate each day.

In a few days the sheep's fleece will be ready to shear with scissors and eat.

from **Kitchen Fun** *by Ray Gibson*

3 Responding to the text

Answer the questions from the , or section.

1 What is the sheep's body made of?

2 What are its legs made of?

3 How many instructions are there to follow?

4 How do you make the sheep's eyes?

1 How often should you water the cress on the cotton wool?

2 Do you need any sticky tape to make the woolly sheep?

3 Would it matter if you followed the instructions in a different order?

4 What is a *fleece*?

1 Why do you need to keep the cotton wool moist?

2 Why do you need to lay the sheep on a plate?

3 Make a list of the words that start each instruction. For example, *pull, cut.*

4 What does the word *shear* mean?

4 Think/pair/share

You're going to use a paper plate to make a mask. Discuss your ideas for a design with your partner.

What do you want your mask to look like?

How will you wear your mask?

What materials will you use?

5 Planning and making

Draw a diagram of your mask. Add labels to show which materials you will use.

Follow the diagram and try to make your mask.

6 Writing instructions

1 Make brief notes of the steps you took to make your mask.

2 Write a list of instructions for making your mask.

3 Swap your instructions with your partner. Do you need to make any changes?

4 Finish your instructions. Display them next to your diagram and mask.

Remember!

- Begin by writing a list of the things you need to make your mask.

- Number each stage of your instructions.

- Use short sentences that start with instruction words.

What I have learned

- I can follow spoken or written instructions.

- I can write instructions for making something.

- I can discuss my work with a partner or in a group.

paper plate

Moo!

stick

3 Stepping Out

In this unit, you'll read and write poems with patterned language on a similar theme.

Street Sounds

This is a sound poem about the noises that different shoes make when you walk in them. Think of the sounds as you read the poem.

I love to hear my feet
as they're walking down the street
in wellies.
Blobble blabble blobble blabble
wobbly wellie feet.

I like to hear Jane's feet
when she's running down the street
in flip-flops.
Slit-slap, slit-slap
slittery slappery feet.

Listen to Mum's feet
parade along the street
in high heels.
Clock clop clock clop
swanky cloppy feet.

Hear my Grandma's feet
as she shuffles down the street
in slippers.
Shlur plock shlur plock
snorey slippery feet.

Jacqueline Brown

1 Responding to the text

Answer the questions from the , or section.

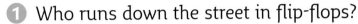

① What sort of shoes is Jane wearing?

② Who is wearing high heels?

③ Write down some other words, which are not used in this poem, that describe the sounds that wellies make.

④ Who shuffles down the street?

① Who runs down the street in flip-flops?

② What sort of shoes is Mum wearing?

③ Who is wearing slippers?

④ What sound do the wellies make?

❶ Who is wearing footwear that is usually worn indoors?

❷ Mum's feet *parade* along the street. What does the poet mean by this?

❸ Which words describe the sounds that Jane's feet make?

❹ Write down four words, which are not used in this poem, that describe how someone moves.

2 Making up a sound poem

Choose another sort of shoe and make up a new verse. Start it like this:

I love to hear my feet
as I ...

We Want to Wear Our Wellies

This is a patterned poem. It is about wearing
wellies – and when not to wear them!

We want to wear our wellies
When it's windy.
We want to wear our wellies
When it's wet.
We want to wear our wellies
When the weather on the telly
Says it's going to be
The warmest day yet.

We want to wear our wellies
Even though our feet get smelly.
We want to wear our wellies
Because they're *red*.
We want to wear our wellies
When it's wet or warm or windy –
But we *never* wear our wellies in bed!

Dave Ward

3 Word work

This sentence uses words that start with the same sound.

We **w**ant to **w**ear our **w**ellies!

Make up some more sentences, using words that start
with the same sound. Here is one to start you off:

We like to play pirates in purple pyjamas.

4 Write/pair/share

Write a new poem about footwear.

Choose any footwear you like.

- Think about how your footwear would look.

- Think about how your feet would sound and move in your footwear.

Choose the best describing words and put them together in two lines, like this:

Flat flippers, flappy flippers,
Flip, flap, flop

Slidy rollers, glidy rollers,
Swish, swash, swoop!

Clumpy clogs, clunky clogs,
Clop, clap, clop.

Make up as many verses as you want to.

Remember!

- Think of interesting words to describe the sounds.

- Think of interesting words to describe how you move.

- Choose some words that start with the same sound.

- You could choose some words that rhyme.

What I have learned

- I can read and perform poems with patterned language.

- I can talk about patterns in poems.

- I can play with interesting words to make patterns.

- I can write a poem with interesting word patterns.

4 A Kiss from a Princess

> In this unit, you'll read and compare different versions of the frog prince story and write a story of your own.

A Kiss from a Princess

This is a modern retelling of the story of the frog prince. It uses a mixture of traditional and modern language.

Once upon a time there lived a princess whose favourite toy was a golden ball. Every day she would go into the gardens of her father's palace and play with her golden ball.

Then one day as the princess stretched out her hands to catch the ball it slipped through her fingers. Across the garden it bounced and PLOP! into the waters of the deep, deep well it went.

How the princess cried! Tears ran down her cheeks until, through her sobs, she heard a small voice say, "Don't cry, Princess. If I get you back your ball what will you give me in return?"

And there, looking at her with his big sad eyes, was a very large frog. "Oh anything, anything!" cried the princess.

"All I want," said the frog, "is to be your companion. I should like to play with you, to eat with you at your table and at night to sleep in your bed."

"Oh I promise, I promise," cried the princess and, straight away, the frog dived into the waters of the deep, deep well and, moments later, returned with the golden ball.

But the princess – who secretly thought frogs were nasty, slimy creatures – snatched the ball and ran back as fast as she could to the palace, leaving the poor frog all on his own.

from **The Story of the Frog Prince** *retold by Margaret Carter*

1 Questions for a princess

In your group, choose someone to play the part of the princess. Put the princess in the "hot seat". Ask her questions about her behaviour. For example:

Why did you break your promise to the frog?

Why was the golden ball so special to you?

What is it that you don't like about frogs?

2 What's it all about?

In pairs, choose a fairytale. Discuss with your partner what happens in your fairytale. Then answer these questions.

- Does this story have a happy ending?

- Who are the good characters in the story? What happens to them in the end?

- Who are the bad characters in the story? What happens to them in the end?

3 What happens next?

1 In your group, tell the last part of *The Story of the Frog Prince.* Use the storyboard to help you.

2 Now write your own ending for the story.
Does it have a happy ending?

The Frog Prince *Continued*

The Princess kissed the frog.
He turned into a prince.
And they lived happily ever after…

adapted from **The Frog Prince Continued** *by Jon Scieszka*

4 Not-so-happy-ever-after

Imagine you're the princess. Write a letter to the king, telling him what it's like being married to the prince. Start your letter like this:

Dear Dad,
I've made a terrible mistake.
It is awful being married to the prince!
For one thing...

Imagine you're the prince. Write a letter to the princess, telling her the things she does that annoy you. Ask her why she won't go to the pond with you any more. Remind her that she doesn't keep her promises.

The Other Frog Prince

In this story, things don't turn out quite the way that you expect!

Once upon a time there was a frog.

One day when he was sitting on his lily pad, he saw a beautiful princess sitting by the pond. He hopped in the water, swam over to her, and poked his head out of the weeds.

"Pardon me, O beautiful princess," he said in his most sad and pathetic voice. "I wonder if you could help me."

The princess was about to jump up and run, but she felt sorry for the frog with the sad and pathetic voice.

So she asked, "What can I do to help you, little frog?"

"Well," said the frog, "I'm not really a frog, but a handsome prince who was turned into a frog by a wicked witch's spell. And the spell can only be broken by the kiss of a beautiful princess."

The princess thought about this for a second, then lifted the frog from the pond and kissed him.

"I was just kidding," said the frog. He jumped back into the pond and the princess wiped the frog slime off her lips. The End.

from **The Stinky Cheese Man and Other Fairly Stupid Tales** by *Jon Scieszka*

5 Planning a puppet show

1 Read the words spoken by the frog and the princess aloud with a partner.

2 Using the spoken words in the story, write a script for a puppet show. For example:

Frog: Pardon me, O beautiful princess, I wonder if you could help me.

Princess: What can I do to help you, little frog?

Frog: Well...

Don't forget to include stage directions for the kiss!

3 Make stick puppets of the frog and the princess. Perform your story as a puppet show.

6 Writing a modern fairytale

Write your own story about a frog prince.

How will it be the same as the traditional story?

- Will a prince be turned into a frog?
- Will the frog look for a princess to kiss him?

How will it be different?

- Perhaps a princess will be turned into a frog.
- Perhaps the frog will turn into something else at the end.

Remember!

- Think of an unexpected ending to surprise the reader.
- Decide whether to use traditional language, modern language or a mixture of both.
- Write in complete sentences.

What I have learned

- I can recognise the elements of a traditional story.
- I can explore different endings.
- I can plan and write a story with traditional story elements and an alternative ending.

Hatched from an Egg

In this unit, you'll look at explanations and flow diagrams, and then present an explanation of your own.

Snake Charm

How do snakes shed their skin?

This explanation is presented as a flow diagram.

As the snake grows bigger, its skin becomes dull, and very tight. It needs to shed its skin. It may take several days to do this. Its eyes become milky and it is nearly blind at this stage, so it hides away from danger.

When the old skin is shed, the eyes are clear and the new skin is bright and shiny.

The snake rubs its mouth on a hard object, such as rock. The first bit of skin peels away. Soon its head emerges from the old skin.

Next, the snake wriggles its way out of the old skin, turning it inside out like a sock.

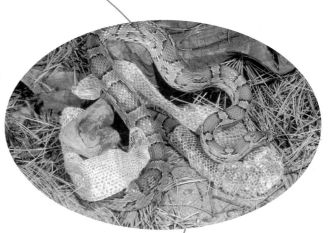

The snake leaves its old skin behind.

1 Responding to the text

Answer the questions from the , or section.

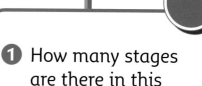

❶ How long does it take a snake to shed its skin?

❷ What happens to the snake's eyes?

❸ What is underneath the snake's old skin?

❶ How many stages are there in this explanation?

❷ Why does a snake need to shed its skin?

❸ What happens to the snake's old skin as the snake wriggles out of it?

❶ What is the sub-heading on page 34?

❷ Why does the snake hide when it's ready to shed its skin?

❸ How does the snake begin to shed its skin?

2 Preparing a presentation

In pairs, plan a presentation to explain how a snake sheds its skin. Use the flow diagram on pages 34 and 35 to help you.

- Point to each picture in the diagram as you describe that stage.

- Speak clearly – you'll need to speak louder and more slowly than usual.

- Look at your audience while you're speaking.

- Practise your presentation, ready to show to your group.

Butterfly Life Cycle

This text tells you about the life cycle of a butterfly.

Butterflies are **insects**. Like other insects, the butterfly has three main parts to its body: the **head**, the **thorax** and the **abdomen**.

thorax

head

abdomen

The caterpillars can eat this plant when they hatch.

The butterfly starts life as an **egg**.

A female butterfly lays many eggs on a plant. The eggs are sticky, which prevents them from falling off. After a while, each egg hatches to produce a **caterpillar**.

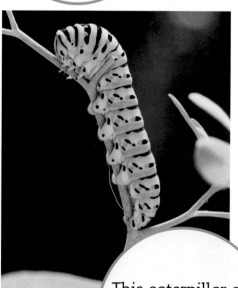

The caterpillar spends most of its time munching on leaves and growing bigger.

When it is fully grown, the caterpillar changes into a **chrysalis**.

This caterpillar can give off a horrible smell to scare away predators.

Another word that means the same as chrysalis is **pupa**.

An amazing transformation takes place inside the chrysalis. The caterpillar changes into a butterfly. This process is called **metamorphosis**. When the butterfly is ready, it breaks open the chrysalis and crawls out.

This is a swallowtail butterfly.

3 Note-making

Make notes about the life cycle of a butterfly.
You'll use them later to make your own flow diagram.

❶ Read through the information carefully.
Look closely at the captions.

❷ Talk about what you've read with your partner.
Was there anything you didn't understand?

❸ Read through the text again.

❹ Make notes about each stage of the life cycle.
You could write a sentence in your own words,
or sketch a picture, for each stage.

Eggs and Chicks

This text explains what happens inside the egg, as a chick grows and then hatches out.

Inside an egg

When an egg is laid, a chick starts to grow inside.

The red spot on the yolk
starts to grow into a chick.

The yolk contains food which
helps the chick to grow.

The chick grows bigger.
The white protects the chick.

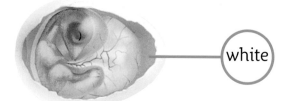

Chicks take from 10 days to 75 days to grow inside an egg.

The chick grows to look like a tiny bird
with a beak, eyes and feet.

A chick cheeps inside its egg.
Its parents can hear its call.

Hatching

When a chick is strong enough, it hatches from its egg.

 egg tooth

1 A chick has a lump on its beak called an egg tooth.

2 It uses its egg tooth to make holes around the shell.

3 The chick pushes the top off the egg, then rests for a while.

4 The chick struggles out of the shell. Its feathers are damp.

The chick's feathers dry and become fluffy.

The chick doesn't need its egg tooth. Soon it drops off.

from **Eggs and Chicks** *by Fiona Patchett*

4 Read/pair/share

In pairs, talk about the section that explains the different stages in the growth of a chicken. Read the descriptions and explain to your partner what is happening in each picture.

What other animals do you know about that start life inside an egg?

5 Think/pair/share

You're going to write an explanation on a different topic. In pairs, talk about:

- what your explanation will be about.

- what the different stages will show.

- how you will organise your explanation.

6 Independent writing

1 Make notes to show the different stages of your explanation.

2 Use your notes to write a list of sentences.

3 Read your explanation. How could you improve it?

Remember!

You could:

- add a heading.

- write a sentence to introduce your explanation.

- use time words such as **first**, **then**, **next** and **finally**.

- use explanation words such as **because**, **so** and **that**.

- add a flow diagram with pictures, captions and arrows.

7 Speaking and listening

Present your explanation or diagram to a partner or small group.

- How well did you explain yourself?

- Did they understand what you were trying to explain?

- How could you improve your explanation?

What I have learned

- I can put sentences and pictures in order, to explain a process.

- I can understand a simple flow chart that explains a process.

- I can use time words and explanation words.

- I can write an explanation and present it to a group.

Delicious Dishes

In this unit, you'll read and write poems that describe different foods.

Hot Food

This poem is about a family eating hot potatoes.

We sit down to eat
and the potato's a bit hot
so I only put a little bit on my fork
and I blow
whooph whooph
until it's cool
just cool
then into the mouth
nice.
And there's my brother
he's doing the same
whooph whooph
into the mouth
nice.
There's my mum
she's doing the same
whooph whooph
into the mouth
nice.

But my dad.
My dad.
What does he do?
He stuffs a great big chunk of potato
into his mouth.
Then
that really does it.
His eyes pop out
he flaps his hands
he blows, he puffs, he yells
he bobs his head up and down
he spits bits of potato
all over his plate
and he turns to us and he says,
"Watch out everybody –
the potato's very hot."

Michael Rosen

1 Role play

Play this game with your group. One of you thinks of a food and pretends to eat it. The others guess what the food is.

Here are some ideas:

- cold ice-cream
- crisp apple
- fluffy candyfloss

Spaghetti! Spaghetti!

This poem about spaghetti uses many interesting describing words.

Spaghetti! spaghetti!
you're wonderful stuff,
I love you, spaghetti,
I can't get enough.
You're covered with sauce
and you're sprinkled with cheese,
spaghetti! spaghetti!
oh, give me some please.

Spaghetti! spaghetti!
piled high in a mound,
you wiggle, you wriggle,
you squiggle around.
There's slurpy spaghetti
all over my plate,
spaghetti! spaghetti!
I think you are great.

Spaghetti! spaghetti!
I love you a lot,
you're slishy, you're sloshy,
delicious and hot.
I gobble you down
oh, I can't get enough
spaghetti! spaghetti!
you're wonderful stuff.

Jack Prelutsky

2 Responding to the text

Answer the questions from the   or 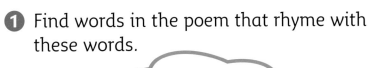 section.

❶ Find words in the poem that rhyme with these words.

> *stuff*   *cheese*
>
> *mound*   *wiggle*
>
> *plate*   *lot*

❷ How many different words can you find that begin with "s"?

❸ How many lines are there in each verse?

❹ What words has the poet used to describe spaghetti?

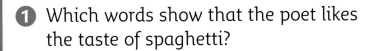

❶ Which words show that the poet likes the taste of spaghetti?

❷ Think of other words that he could have used to show he likes the taste, for example, *yummy*.

❸ Count the number of syllables in each line of the poem. Is there a pattern?

❹ Is the rhythm the same for each verse?

47

3 Think/pair/share

In pairs, think about what your favourite food looks like, feels like and tastes like. Talk about different words you could use to describe it.

crisp
sharp

rough
lumpy

soft
smooth

firm
waxy

rosy
velvety

nutty
sweet-smelling

hard
crunchy

clean
shiny

fresh
mouth-watering

sour
bitter

sweet
juicy

4 Write/pair/share

Draw a spider diagram for your food. Here is an example.
Discuss your diagram with a friend.

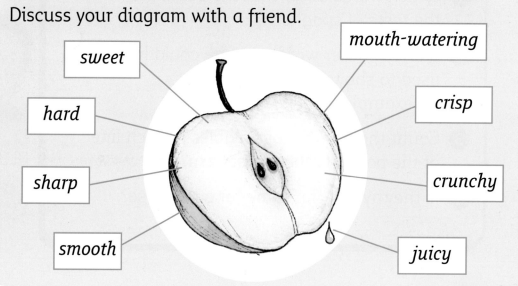

sweet

mouth-watering

hard

crisp

sharp

crunchy

smooth

juicy

5 Independent writing

Now try writing a poem about your favourite food.

You could use some of the ideas from the poems you've read in this unit.

Remember!

- Choose interesting words to describe the taste, feel and smell.

- Choose words that sound good together.

- Your poem doesn't have to rhyme.

- Practise saying your poem aloud to hear how it sounds.

What I have learned

- I can think of interesting describing words.

- I can talk about rhyme and rhythm in poems.

- I can write a poem with describing words.

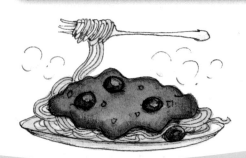

Jill Murphy

In this unit, you'll read and compare two stories by the author and illustrator, Jill Murphy. You'll read information about her and write a review.

The Last Noo-Noo

Marlon is a monster with a bad habit. His granny says he's too old for a dummy but Marlon isn't ready to give up his noo-noos just yet!

Marlon sat on the floor watching TV. Marlon's granny sat in the armchair, watching Marlon.

"He's getting too old for that dummy," she said sternly to Marlon's mum.

"It's a noo-noo," said Marlon.

"He calls it a noo-noo," explained Marlon's mum.

"Well, what*ever* he calls it," said Marlon's granny, "he looks like an idiot with that stupid great *thing* stuck in his mouth all the time."

"He doesn't have it *all* the time," soothed Marlon's mum. "Only at night or if he's a bit tired. He's a bit tired now – aren't you, pet?"

"Mmmmm," said Marlon.

"His teeth will start sticking out," warned Marlon's granny.

"Monsters' teeth stick out anyway," observed Marlon.

"Don't answer back," said Marlon's granny. "You should just throw them *all* away," she continued. "At this rate he'll be starting *school* with a dummy. At this rate he'll be starting *work* with a dummy. You'll just have to be firm with him."

"Well," said Marlon's mum, "I am *thinking* about it. We'll start next week, won't we Marlon? Now you're a big boy, we'll just get rid of all those silly noo-noos, won't we?"

"No," said Marlon.

"You see!" said Marlon's granny. "One word from you and he does as he likes."

There was no doubt about it. Marlon was a hopeless case.

from **The Last Noo-Noo** *by Jill Murphy*

1 Role play

In groups of three, role play Marlon, his mum and his granny talking about his noo-noos.

 **Marlon:** Explain why you won't give up your noo-noos. What is it you like about them? Is there anything Mum and Granny could do to persuade you to give them up?

 Mum: Speak sternly to Marlon. Tell him he is much too big for noo-noos and he will have to give them up whether he likes it or not.

 Granny: Explain why Marlon should give up his noo-noos. Give Mum some advice about how to be firm with him.

The Worst Witch

*Jill Murphy has written many stories about a young witch
called Mildred Hubble. However hard she tries, Mildred can't
seem to stay out of trouble.*

It had taken Mildred several weeks of falling off and
crashing before she could ride the broomstick reasonably
well, and it looked as though her kitten was going to have
the same trouble. When she put it on the end of the stick, it
just fell off without even trying to hold on. After many
attempts, Mildred picked up her kitten and gave it a shake.

"Listen!" she said severely. "I think I shall have to call you Stupid. You don't even *try* to hold on. Everyone else is all right – look at all your friends."

The kitten gazed at her sadly and licked her nose with its rough tongue.

"Oh, come on," said Mildred, softening her voice. "I'm not really angry with you. Let's try again."

And she put the kitten back on the broomstick, from which it fell with a thud.

Maud was having better luck. Her kitten was hanging on grimly upside down.

"Oh well," laughed Maud. "It's a start."

"Mine's useless," said Mildred, sitting on the broomstick for a rest.

"Never mind," Maud said. "Think how hard it must be for them to hang on by their claws."

An idea flashed into Mildred's head, and she dived into the school, leaving her kitten chasing a leaf along the ground and the broomstick still patiently hovering. She came out carrying her satchel which she hooked over the end of the broom and then bundled the kitten into it. The kitten's astounded face peeped out of the bag as Mildred flew delightedly round the yard.

"Look, Maud!" she called from ten feet up in the air.

"That's cheating!" said Maud, looking at the satchel.

Mildred flew back and landed on the ground laughing.

"I don't think H.B. will approve," said Maud doubtfully.

"Quite right, Maud," an icy voice behind them said. "Mildred, my dear, possibly it would be even easier with handlebars and a saddle."

Mildred blushed.

"I'm sorry, Miss Hardbroom," she muttered. "It doesn't balance very well – my kitten, so … I thought … perhaps …" Her voice trailed away under Miss Hardbroom's stony glare and Mildred unhooked her satchel and turned the bewildered kitten on to the ground.

from **The Worst Witch** *by Jill Murphy*

2 Responding to the text

Answer the questions from the , or section.

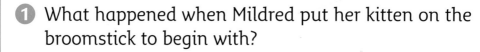

1. What happened when Mildred put her kitten on the broomstick to begin with?

2. What name did Mildred think of calling her kitten?

3. What did Mildred fetch from the school?

4. How did she get her kitten to stay on the broomstick?

1. How long had it taken Mildred to learn how to ride her broomstick?

2. What did Maud think of Mildred's idea?

3. What did Maud mean when she said "I don't think H.B. will approve"?

4. Why did Mildred blush?

1. Why was Mildred cross with her kitten?

2. How did Maud's kitten manage to stay on the broomstick?

3. What did Mildred's teacher think of her idea?

4. What did Miss Hardbroom mean when she said "Possibly it would have been even easier with handlebars and a saddle"?

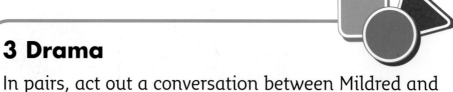

3 Drama

In pairs, act out a conversation between Mildred and Miss Hardbroom. What do you think Miss Hardbroom will have to say to Mildred about her unusual way of keeping her kitten on the broomstick? How will Mildred explain her behaviour?

Jill Murphy

The author and illustrator, Jill Murphy, started drawing pictures, writing stories and putting books together before she was six years old. Here she explains what she was like at school, and where she got the idea for Mildred Hubble.

I can't remember a time when I wasn't writing stories and drawing pictures. I was busily making little books before I even went to school.

I was actually rather a good child at primary school, where I showed such early promise, but when I went up to the grammar school at eleven, I completely changed character and became exactly like Mildred Hubble, which is why I made her the heroine of my first book, *The Worst Witch*.

Writing and illustrating my own books was the only thing I ever wanted to do and I did it! You can't beat the feeling of joy which comes with that!

from **Author profile** *by* **The Book Trust**

Questionnaire for Jill Murphy

What was your favourite subject when you were at school?
English

What was your worst subject?
Maths, science and games

What is your favourite food?
Beans on toast, with cheese melted on top

What is your favourite own book?
Peace at Last

What is your favourite own character?
Mildred in *The Worst Witch*

If you could travel back in time, what period would you go to?
Tudor England

from Author profile *by The Book Trust*

4 Responding to the text

Answer the questions from the   or section.

1 What was Jill Murphy's favourite subject at school?

2 What is Jill Murphy's favourite food?

3 Do you think Jill Murphy enjoys her work?

4 Jill Murphy illustrates her own books. What does an *illustrator* do?

5 What question would you ask Jill Murphy if you met her?

1 What sort of child was Jill Murphy at primary school?

2 In what way did she change when she moved school?

3 What is the only thing Jill Murphy ever wanted to do?

4 Which of her own books does she like best?

5 Speaking and listening

Work in pairs. Ask each other these questions and note down the answers.

- Which of the two stories by Jill Murphy did you enjoy more?

- Which character did you find most interesting? Explain your reasons.

Now ask each other the questions that Jill Murphy was asked. Give your own answers.

Think of two more questions to ask.

6 Writing a review

Write a review about one of the stories you have read.

- Say what type of story it is.

- Write a little bit about what happens – but don't give too much away!

- Who do you think would like to read the story?

Try not to use words such as *good* and *boring*. Think of more interesting words to use.

7 Writing your own story

Write an adventure story of your own, starring Mildred Hubble and her kitten.

- Where will the story be set?

- How will Mildred get into trouble?

- Who will help her?

Who?

Where?

How?

Remember!

- Include some conversation between characters.

- Think about how the characters behave in Jill Murphy's story and make them recognisable in your adventure story.

- Use interesting words.

What I have learned

- I can talk about an author and the type of books they write.

- I can listen to others in a group and express my own ideas and opinions.

- I can write a story, using a character from a story I have read.

From A to Z

In this unit, you'll look at a range of alphabetical texts. You'll make a mini-glossary and write definitions for a class dictionary.

A Glossary of Bird Words

*A **glossary** is a mini-dictionary. It's a list of special words, and their meanings, linked to a topic. Lots of information books have glossaries.*

cygnet – a baby swan

duckling – a baby duck

egg tooth – the part of a chick's beak which it uses to break the egg shell

hatch – when a chick breaks out of its egg through the shell

nest – a place that birds build to keep their eggs and chicks safe

speckled – covered with little dots that make a pattern

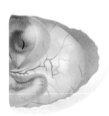

yolk – the yellow part in the middle of an egg. It helps the chick to grow.

from **Eggs and Chicks** *by* **Fiona Patchett**

1 Responding to the text

Answer the questions from the , or section.

1 What are the words in the glossary about?

2 What is a baby duck called?

3 What is a *cygnet*?

4 What is a nest used for?

1 Why are the words listed in alphabetical order?

2 What does a chick use an *egg tooth* for?

3 What is a *yolk*?

4 Why do you think words such as *egg* and *chick* have not been included in this glossary?

1 Whereabouts in a book would you expect to find a glossary? Why?

2 Why do you think the word *speckled* is included in the glossary for *Eggs and Chicks*?

3 How is a glossary different from a dictionary?

4 What other words might you include in this glossary?

2 Speaking and listening

Look for glossaries and word lists in other information books. Answer these questions in pairs.

- Where in the book does the glossary or word list appear?

- How is it presented?

- Is it a useful list of words?

- How many of the words listed do you already know?

- Which words are new to you?

3 Making a mini-glossary

You're going to make your own mini-glossary.

Make a glossary of useful words about a class topic or a non-fiction book you've read. Write a simple definition for each word.

- Choose words that you think other readers may not know the meaning of.

- Test out your definitions on a friend.

Make a glossary of names for baby animals.

Start by putting these animal names into alphabetical order:

chick kitten puppy cub duckling foal lamb joey piglet

Write a simple definition for each word. The first one has been done for you.

chick   a baby bird

J words

A dictionary tells you what a word means and how to spell it.
The words in a dictionary are listed in alphabetical order.

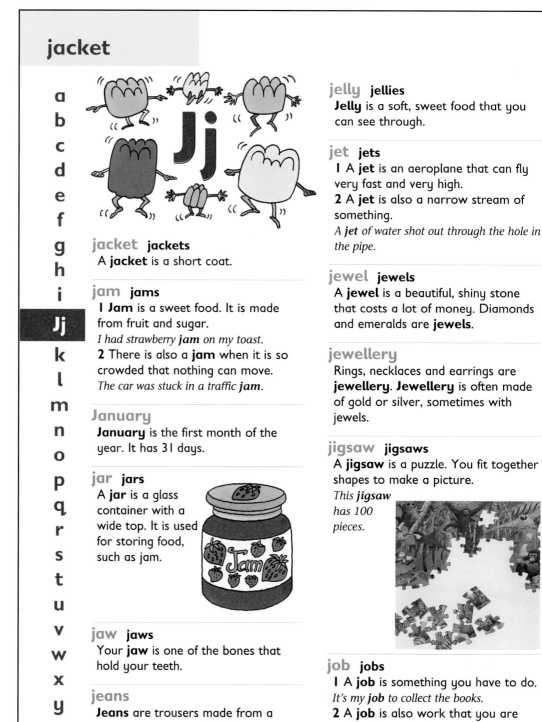

jacket

a b c d e f g h i **Jj** k l m n o p q r s t u v w x y z

jacket jackets
A **jacket** is a short coat.

jam jams
1 **Jam** is a sweet food. It is made from fruit and sugar.
I had strawberry jam on my toast.
2 There is also a **jam** when it is so crowded that nothing can move.
The car was stuck in a traffic jam.

January
January is the first month of the year. It has 31 days.

jar jars
A **jar** is a glass container with a wide top. It is used for storing food, such as jam.

jaw jaws
Your **jaw** is one of the bones that hold your teeth.

jeans
Jeans are trousers made from a strong cotton material. They are often blue. (See page 176.)

jelly jellies
Jelly is a soft, sweet food that you can see through.

jet jets
1 A **jet** is an aeroplane that can fly very fast and very high.
2 A **jet** is also a narrow stream of something.
A jet of water shot out through the hole in the pipe.

jewel jewels
A **jewel** is a beautiful, shiny stone that costs a lot of money. Diamonds and emeralds are **jewels**.

jewellery
Rings, necklaces and earrings are **jewellery**. **Jewellery** is often made of gold or silver, sometimes with jewels.

jigsaw jigsaws
A **jigsaw** is a puzzle. You fit together shapes to make a picture.
This jigsaw has 100 pieces.

job jobs
1 A **job** is something you have to do.
It's my job to collect the books.
2 A **job** is also work that you are paid to do.
My mum has a job as a bus driver.

just

join **joins, joining, joined**
1 When you **join** things, you put them together.

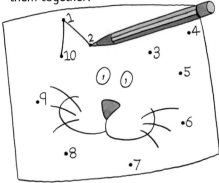

2 If you **join** a club, you become a member of it.
Sophie has joined the swimming club.

joint **joints**
A **joint** is a part of the body where two bones fit together.
Your finger joints are called knuckles.

joke **jokes**
A **joke** is something that you say to make people laugh.

journey **journeys**
If you go on a **journey**, you travel from one place to another.

jug **jugs**
A **jug** is a container for holding liquids. It has a handle and a lip for pouring.

juice **juices**
Juice is the liquid that can be squeezed out of fruit.
I drink orange juice at breakfast.

July
July is the seventh month of the year. It has 31 days.

jump **jumps, jumping, jumped**
You **jump** when you move yourself into the air.
Tim jumped off the wall.

jumper **jumpers**
A **jumper** is a piece of clothing with sleeves. You wear it on the top half of your body to keep you warm.

June
June is the sixth month of the year. It has 30 days.

jungle **jungles**
A **jungle** is a thick forest in a hot country.

just
If something has **just** happened, it happened a very short time ago.
I just got to school a minute ago.

a
b
c
d
e
f
g
h
i
Jj
k
l
m
n
o
p
q
r
s
t
u
v
w
x
y
z

from **Collins First School Dictionary**

4 Responding to the text

Answer the questions from the , or section.

1 What is the first word in this dictionary that begins with "j"?

2 What is a *jigsaw*?

3 What is a *jar* made of?

4 Which word comes after *jeans*?

1 What is the guide word on these pages?

2 Which headwords begin with a capital letter?

3 What is the plural word for *jelly*?

4 What is the special name for an aeroplane that can fly very fast and very high?

1 What are jeans made of?

2 Which four headwords on these pages each have two definitions?

3 What letter do the words on the previous page of this dictionary begin with?

4 Would these pages appear in the first or the second half of the dictionary?

5 Dictionary races

This is a game for three or more players.

Each player needs a dictionary. Take turns to choose and call out a word for the other players to find. The other players race to see who can be the first to find the word in their dictionary and read out the definition.

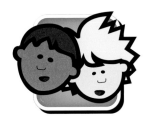

6 Building a class dictionary

In a group, make a dictionary of words linked to a topic that has been agreed on by the whole class.

1 With a partner, make a list of useful words to do with the topic. Then put the words in alphabetical order.

2 Look up some topic words in a dictionary. Think about what the dictionary tells you – and what it doesn't. Discuss the definitions with a partner.

3 In your group, write simple definitions for each of your topic words. Decide together how you will work as a group.

- How will you complete the task?
- Who will do what?
- Make sure everybody is included.

Remember!

- List the topic words in alphabetical order.
- Try out your definitions on a friend.
- You could add the plural for each of your topic words.

What I have learned

- I can use dictionaries and glossaries to find definitions.
- I can use indexes to find information.
- I can write simple definitions for a class dictionary of special interest words.

9 Playing with Words

In this unit, you'll read jokes, funny poems, riddles and tongue-twisters. You'll play with words to make up some funny poems of your own.

Telling Jokes

Words can be very funny.

> Why did the football player wear a bib?
> *Because he was always dribbling.*

This joke is funny because the word *dribbling* has two meanings. Do you know what they are?

> Where would you take a sick pony?
> *To a horsepital.*

An invented spelling makes this joke funny. The invented word is a cross between *horse* and *hospital*.

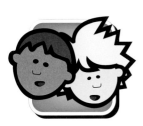

1 What's so funny?

In pairs, match these questions and answers to find some funny jokes. Talk about what it is that makes each joke funny.

Cats, because they are very mewsical.

Why did the doll blush?

Chewsday.

On which day do monsters eat people?

Which pets are the best singers?

Because she saw the teddy bear.

2 Hard lines

Try making up your own tongue-twister. Use words that sound similar or start with the same letters. Try repeating your tongue-twister again and again. For example:

She sells seashells on the seashore.

The shells she sells are seashells, I'm sure.

How many times can you say it without making a mistake?

3 Get in a twist!

Look at the tongue-twister in the  ,  or  section.
Practise reading it aloud.
Try not to get your tongue in a tangle!

Breakfast for One

Hot thick crusty buttery toast
Buttery toasty thick hot crust
Crusty buttery hot thick toast
Crusty thick hot toasty butter
Thick hot buttery crusty toast
Toasty buttery hot thick crust
Hot buttery thick crusty toast –

With marmalade is how I like it most!

Judith Nicholls

Teatime

Take two teaspoons, take two teacups,
Take two teabags too,
Tip the teabags in the teapot,
Time for tea for two.

Valerie Bloom

A Proper Cup of Coffee

All I want is a proper cup of coffee
Made in a proper copper coffee-pot.

Anon

Teaser

What kind of ants
tear down trees?
What kind of ants
roll in mud
to take their ease?
What kind of ants
have four knees?
What kind of ants
flap their ears
in the breeze?
What kind of ants
spell their name
with two "e"s?
Sh! Don't tell.
It's a tease.

Answer: elephants

Tony Mitton

4 Responding to the text

Answer the questions from the or section.

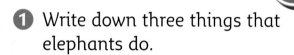

1. Write down three things that elephants do.

2. How many words can you find that rhyme with *tease*?

3. How many questions does the poet ask in this poem?

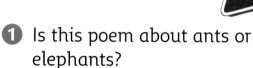

1. Is this poem about ants or elephants?

2. What other animals can you think of that spell their name with two "e"s?

5 Finding words

Find as many words as you can, using only letters from the word *elephant*. You can use any of the letters, in any order, but only as many times as they appear in *elephant*.

For example, *ten, eel, tale...*

6 Planning and writing a riddle poem

1. Think of a word with a smaller word inside it, for example gi**ant**s.

2. Think of a question that gives a clue to the bigger word. For example: *What kind of ants eat small boys?* (giants) *What kind of keys swing from trees?* (monkeys)

3. Try out your riddles on a partner. Write down your best ideas.

4. Use your ideas to make a poem!

Remember!

- Start a new line for each question.
- Put a question mark at the end of each question.

What I have learned

- I can talk about what makes a joke funny.
- I know that a tongue-twister uses lots of words that start with the same sound.
- I know that a riddle is a word puzzle.
- I can make up a silly poem by playing with words and ideas.

Turning the Page

> In this unit, you'll read a whole story, in chapters, by Vivian French. Then you'll use one of her characters in a chapter of your own.

Mountain Mona

Mountain Mona is a funny story told in four chapters. It's about a goat who doesn't think she is good at anything except growing flowers. Then she meets a lion who tells her why she isn't quite like other goats.

Chapter 1

Mona was a goat. She lived at the top of a mountain with her brother, her sister and her mother.

Her brother was good at jumping.

Her sister was good at leaping.

Her mother was good at climbing and scrambling.

Mona didn't think she was good at ANYTHING … except growing flowers.

Mona grew big yellow sunflowers – huge yellow sunflowers that nodded in the sunshine.

Mona loved them. She fed them and watered them.

She watched them grow … and she smiled.

"Mona," said her brother, "goats don't grow flowers. JUMPING is what goats do. If a fierce lion comes along, goats must JUMP out of the way. Jumping is easy peasy. Watch me jump over this bush!"

Mona looked round.

"What bush?" she asked.

"THIS bush," replied her brother.

"Oh," said Mona. "I thought it was a rock."

Mona's brother jumped over the bush.

"There!" he said. "Now you try!"

Mona tried …

"OW!" she said.

OW!

"You should look where you're jumping," said her brother.

"I did!" Mona replied, and she went to see her sunflowers.

Chapter 2

"Mona," said her sister, "goats don't grow flowers. LEAPING is what goats do. If a fierce lion comes along, goats must LEAP out of the way. Leaping is easy peasy. Watch me leap from rock to rock!"

Mona looked round.

"What rocks?" she asked.

"THESE rocks," said her sister.

"Oh," said Mona. "I thought they were bushes."

Mona's sister leapt from rock to rock.

"There!" she said. "Now you try."

Mona tried …

"OW!" she said.

"You should look where you're leaping," said her sister.

"I DID!" replied Mona, and she went to see her sunflowers.

"Mona," said her mother, "why don't you try climbing and scrambling?"

Mona sighed a huge sigh.

"All right," she said. "I'll try."

Mona began to climb, but she fell on a thistle.

She tried to scramble, but she bumped her nose.

"It's no good," she said. "I can't do the things other goats can. Besides, I don't LIKE jumping … or leaping … or climbing … or scrambling.

And I don't care about fierce lions either.

AND I don't like living on the top of a mountain. Mountains make me dizzy."

Mona stomped off down the mountain.

from Mountain Mona *by Vivian French (Collins Big Cat)*

1 Responding to the text

Answer the questions from the , or  section.

1 Who are the other members of Mona's family?

2 What is Mona good at?

3 How does Mona look after the sunflowers?

4 Why doesn't Mona like living on the top of a mountain?

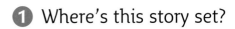

1 Where's this story set?

2 Find a word in Chapter 1 that means the same as *jumping*.

3 Why does Mona's brother think she should take up jumping?

4 What words would you use to describe Mona?

1 Mona's mother was good at scrambling and climbing. How is *scrambling* different from *climbing*?

2 What happens when Mona tries to jump over the bush?

3 Why do you think Mona keeps trying to do what her family suggest, even though she keeps getting hurt?

Mountain Mona – continued

This is how the story continues.

Chapter 3

At the bottom of the mountain was a lion.

A great big fierce lion.

A great big fierce lion wearing spectacles.

A great big fierce lion wearing spectacles, who opened his mouth WIDE and showed his SHARP teeth.

Mona didn't move. She stood quite still and smiled.

"Excuse me," said the lion, "but please don't smile. PLEASE run away. And please do it NOW!"

"Why?" said Mona.

"Because," said the lion, "that's what goats do. They run away. Then big fierce lions chase them."

Mona frowned. "Are you a lion?"

"YES," said the lion. "What did you think I was?"

"Well," said Mona, "I thought you were a sunflower."

"A SUNFLOWER?" The lion looked angry. "I'm a BIG FIERCE LION!"

Mona looked at the lion more closely.

"I thought you were a BIG sunflower," she said.

The lion sat down. "This is terrible," he said.

"How can I scare anyone if I look like a sunflower?"

Mona thought hard.

"Maybe I'm no good at being scared," she said, quietly.

"After all, I'm no good at jumping or leaping or climbing or scrambling. Maybe I'm no good at being scared either."

"Hmmm," growled the lion. "But …" He began to look excited. "What if it's something else? What if you're no good at SEEING things?"

"What do you mean?" asked Mona.

"You thought I was a sunflower, didn't you? Here, try on my spectacles!"

"All right," said Mona.

She put on the spectacles.

Chapter 4

"WOW!" Mona said.

"WOW! I can see for MILES!"

She looked all around.

"WOW! WOW! WOW!"

"Stop saying WOW," said the lion, "and look at me."

Mona looked at the lion.

"WOW," she said, and she sprang in the air.
"You ARE a big fierce lion."

And Mona jumped …

… and leapt

… and climbed

… and scrambled all the way to the very top

of the mountain.

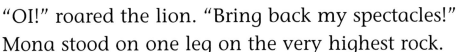

"OI!" roared the lion. "Bring back my spectacles!"

Mona stood on one leg on the very highest rock.

"You look MUCH fiercer without them!"

she shouted, loudly.

"Oh," purred the lion. "Do I?"

And he slipped

… and he staggered

… and he fell over thistles and bushes,

all the way back down to his cave.

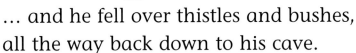

Mona stood on her rock and shouted to her brother, her sister and her mother.

"Look at me!" she said. "I can jump! And I can leap! And climb! And scramble! I can do all the things goats are meant to do!"

"WOW!" said her brother and sister.

"Good," said her mother. "But there's something else you're VERY good at."

"Is there?" asked Mona. "What's that?"

"Getting rid of big fierce lions!" said her mother, with a huge smile.

from Mountain Mona *by Vivian French (Collins Big Cat)*

2 Speaking and listening

Pretend you're Mona, telling the story to her friends. Explain how you scared away a great big fierce lion. Use the story map to help you.

Mountain Mona

The Leaping Rocks

Mona's Rock

Mona's Sunflowers

The Lion's Cave

The Scrambling Rocks

The Jumping Bushes

3 Planning your own story

1 Choose a main character.

2 Choose some other characters.

3 Choose a story setting.

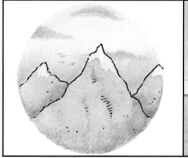

4 Think of a problem to explore in your story.
Write down the main events.

Beginning ⇨ Problem ⇨ How the problem is sorted out ⇨ Ending

5 You can always change your mind once you start your story but it helps to start with a plan.

4 Writing your own story

Use your plan to write your own story.

Remember!

- Describe the characters and setting

- Write your story in the past tense.

- Include some conversation between characters.

- Avoid overusing words such as **said**.

What I have learned

- I can read and talk about a longer story.

- I can plan and write a new story about a familiar character.

Poke Your Tongue Out

In this unit, you'll look for information about mouths, make notes and write your own report.

What Are Mouths For?

This text explores the amazing ways that different animals use their mouths to bite, chew, warn, hunt and even wash.

Mouths are for eating, drinking and speaking.

Mouths are for tasting, biting and licking.

Mouths are for sipping, chewing and smiling.

Mouths are for SHOUTING, whispering and *YAWNING*.

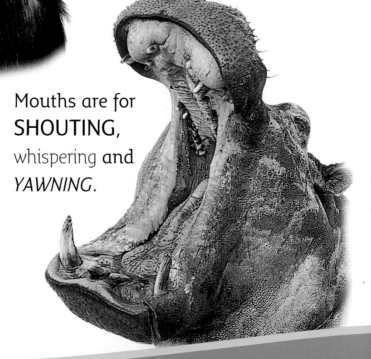

Mouths are for singing, blowing and kissing.

Mum says, "Don't stick your tongue out."

But a chameleon (kuh-MEEL-yun) flicks out a long tongue that sticks to an insect like flypaper.

A cat uses her rough tongue like a comb to lick and clean her fur.

Sharp shooter

A chameleon's tongue shoots out like a spring. Catching insects is tricky. Baby chameleons often miss.

A gecko can clean his own eyes with his long tongue.

Dad says, "Don't stand there with your mouth wide open."

Try telling that to a snake who is trying to swallow an egg...

or a howler monkey who's warning others not to come too close...

or a hyena who won't stop laughing.

The hyena's laugh is no joking matter. Hyenas make this sound when they hunt and kill their prey.

Mighty biters

Spotted hyenas have very strong jaws that can crush and chew large bones and horns. Even lions can't do this.

Mum says, "Brush your teeth."
But some sharks don't need toothbrushes. Small fish clean their teeth for them.

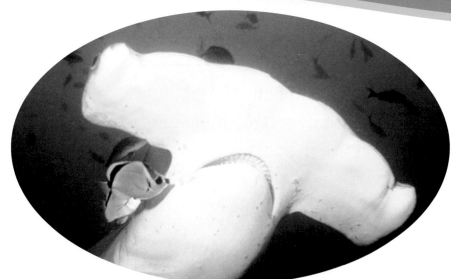

A hamster's strong teeth never stop growing. So he doesn't care about tooth decay.

A turtle never has to worry about losing her teeth because she hasn't got any!
Instead, the edges of her jaws are hard and bony.

Underwater fishing

An alligator snapping turtle's tongue looks like a worm. When she opens her mouth, fish think they see dinner. They swim in and get snapped up!

from **Munching, Crunching, Sniffing and Snooping** *by* **Brian Moses**

1 Write/pair/share

Read the text. In pairs, make a list of things that mouths are used for. When you have finished, show your list to another pair and compare your findings.

2 Responding to the text

Answer the questions from the , or 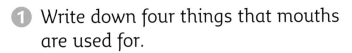 section.

1. Write down four things that mouths are used for.

2. How does a chameleon catch an insect?

3. What does a cat use to clean its fur?

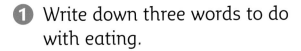

1. Write down three words to do with eating.

2. How do you think small fish help to clean a shark's teeth?

3. How does a turtle bite its food?

1. Write down three things humans do with their mouths that animals do not.

2. What sound does a hyena make when hunting its prey?

3. How do you think hamsters prevent their teeth from getting too long?

How We Taste

This text explains how your sense of taste allows you to try out lots of different flavours.

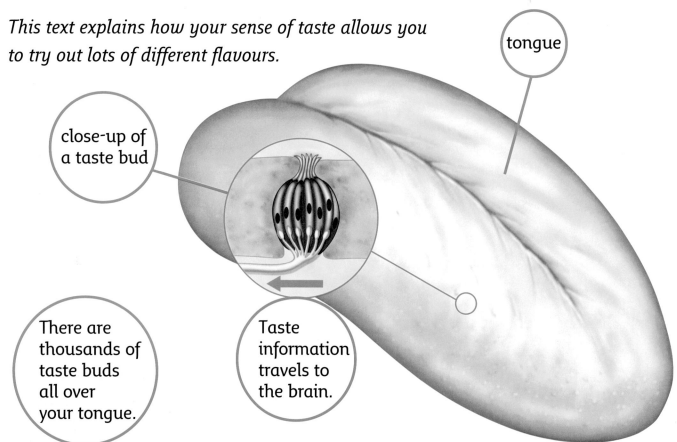

tongue

close-up of a taste bud

There are thousands of taste buds all over your tongue.

Taste information travels to the brain.

Your tongue is covered with lots of tiny bumps called **taste buds**. When your tongue touches food, **information** about that food travels to your brain.

Your mouth makes a liquid called **saliva**. When food is too dry, your mouth makes more saliva. This makes it easier to taste and to eat.

Saliva helps you to swallow dry food like crackers.

Taste and smell

The senses of taste and smell are linked.
If you like the smell of a food or drink, you
will probably like the taste of it, too.

With a cold and a blocked nose, it is difficult
to smell and taste. As people grow older, they
start to lose their senses of taste and smell.

from **Our senses: Taste** *by Kay Woodward*

3 Responding to the text

Answer the questions from the or section.

❶ What part of your body do you *smell* with?

❷ What part of your body do you *taste* with?

❸ Write down two foods that you like the taste of.

❹ Write down two foods that you don't like the taste of.

❶ What are the tiny bumps on your tongue called?

❷ What is saliva and how does it help you?

❸ Which other sense is the sense of smell linked to?

❹ What happens to the sense of taste as you grow older?

❺ There are five senses. Find out what the other senses are.

4 Speaking and listening

You are going to take part in a presentation on *Mouths and the Sense of Taste*. Plan your part of the presentation with your group. Think about:

- a title for your part of the presentation.
- what you want to talk about.
- how you'll work together as a group.
- what jobs each person will do.

Practise your presentation, ready to show to the class.

Remember!

- Make short notes about what you want to say.
- Stand up straight and look at your audience.
- Speak loudly and slowly.

5 Think/pair/share

Read the menu.

Which day do you think has the best meal?

Everytown Primary School – Lunch Menu

	First course	Side dishes	Second course	Drink
Monday:	fish fingers veggie nuggets	All meals come with vegetables or side salad.	fruit scone with jam	water, fruit juice or hot chocolate
Tuesday:	jacket potato with tuna jacket potato with beans		fruit rice pudding	
Wednesday:	pasta with mince pasta with tomato sauce		fruit sponge and custard	

Plan a menu for Thursday, using foods from different food groups.

How will you present your menu?

6 Writing a report

Write a report about eating and drinking, including some of the facts you've learned during this unit. Make notes from non-fiction books and other resources and put the information into your own words.

Remember!

- Think of a fun title, such as **Open Wide!**
- Use sub-headings to organise your information.
- Include some pictures with captions.
- Decide whether a diagram would be helpful.

What I have learned

- I can use non-fiction reports to find information and make notes for a presentation.
- I can write a report and present information in different ways.